The Tragedie of Mariam, the Faire Queene of Jewry by Lady Elizabeth Cary

Elizabeth Tanfield was born in 1585 or 1586 at Burford Priory in Oxfordshire, the only child of Sir Lawrence Tanfield and Elizabeth Symondes. Her father was a lawyer, who later became a judge and the Lord Chief Baron of the Exchequer. Her parents encouraged their daughter's love of reading and learning, although her mother forbade the servants from giving Elizabeth candles to read by at night.

At age five Elizabeth's parents employed a French teacher for her. Within weeks the young child was speaking fluently and would later instruct herself in Spanish, Italian, Latin, Hebrew, and Transylvanian. Her accomplishments as a scholar was acknowledged by such luminaries as Michael Drayton and John Davies in works they dedicated to her.

When she was fifteen, her father arranged for her to marry Sir Henry Cary (later Viscount Falkland). When she finally moved into her husband's home, she was told by her mother-in-law that she was forbidden to read. Unperturbed Elizabeth began to write poetry in her spare time.

After seven years of marriage the now Lord and Lady Falkland began their family; they would go on to have a total of eleven children.

Elizabeth believed that poetry was the highest literary form. Most of her poetry has been lost but evidence of her poetic talent can be seen in her surviving plays. Her play 'The Tragedy of Mariam, the Fair Queen of Jewry' (1613) was written in iambic pentameter with the use of couplets throughout and the use of irony. It was the first English play to be written by a woman.

In 1622 her husband was appointed Lord Deputy of Ireland and Elizabeth went with him to Dublin. There she socialized with prominent local Catholics and patronized Catholic writers.

In 1625 Elizabeth was disinherited by her father just before he died for using part of her jointure to meet the debts of her eldest son, Lucius and to help pay for her husband's lands in Ireland. The same year she returned from Ireland and publicly announced her conversion to Catholicism. This resulted in her husband's attempt (it was unsuccessful) to divorce her. Despite several orders of the Privy Council, he refused her a maintenance in an effort to force her to recant. He also denied her access to their children but she eventually gained custody over her daughters.

Elizabeth wrote 'The History of the Life, Reign, and Death of Edward II' in 1626/27. This was a political fable based on historical events. The story tells of King Edward II and his powerful favorites Gaveston and Spencer. The play is an analogy for King Charles, who in the 1620s was in conflict with Parliament about the power granted to the Duke of Buckingham. Elizabeth was in constant contact with Buckingham and his family and writing the play may have been her way to acknowledge his help and efforts.

Her husband died in 1633, and she sought to regain custody of her sons. It appeared she kidnapped them and was forced to appear before the Star Chamber to answer for this.

In 1634 her daughters Elizabeth, Mary, Lucy and Anne were accepted into the Catholic faith by John Fursdon, their mother's confessor. This was reported to King Charles I and he had the four girls removed from their mother's house and taken to Great Tew, which had been inherited by her son, Lucius, and now the new Viscount Falkland.

By the end of Elizabeth's life her mission to convert her children to Catholicism had become partially successful; four of her daughters went on to become Benedictine nuns, and one of her sons joined the priesthood.

In 1639, Elizabeth Cary, Lady Falkland died in London. She is buried in Henrietta Maria's Chapel in Somerset House.

Index of Contents

TO DIANAES EARTHLIE DEPUTESSE, and my worthy Sister, Mistris Elizabeth Carye

WHen cheerfull Phœbus his full course hath run,
His sisters fainter beames our harts doth cheere:
So your faire Brother is to mee the Sunne,
And you his Sister as my Moone appeare.

You are my next belov'd, my second Friend,
For when my Phœbus absence makes it Night,
Whilst to th' Antipodes his beames do bend,
From you my Phœbe, shines my second Light.

Hee like to SOL, cleare-sighted, constant, free,
You LUNA-like, unspotted, chast, divine:
Hee shone on Sicily, you destin'd bee,
T'illumine the now obscurde Palestine.
My first was consecrated to Apollo,
My second to DIANA now shall follow.

E.C.

Herod, King of Judea.
Doris, his first Wife.
Mariam, his second Wife.
Salome, Herods Sister.
Antipater his sonne by Salome.
Alexandra, Mariams mother.
Silleus, Prince of Arabia.
Constabarus, husband to Salome.
Pheroras, Herods Brother.
Graphina, his Love.
Babus first Sonne.
Babus second Sonne.
Annanell, the high Priest.
Sohemus, a Counseller to Herod.
Nuntio.
Bu, another Messenger.
Chorus, a Companie of Jewes.

THE ARGUMENT

Herod the sonne of Antipater, (an Idumean,) having crept by the favor of the Romanes, into the Jewish Monarchie, married Mariam the daughter of Hircanus, the rightfull King and Priest, and for her (besides her high blood, being of singular beautie) hee reputiated Doris, his former Wife, by whome hee had Children.

This Mariam had a Brother called Aristobolus, and next him and Hircanus his Graund-father, Herod in his Wife's right had the best title. Therefore to remoove them, he charged the first with treason: and put him to death; and drowned the second under colour of sport. Alexandra, Daughter to the one, and Mother to the other, accused him for their deaths before Anthony.

So when hee was forc'te to goe answere this Accusation at Rome, he left the custodie of his wife to Josephus his Uncle, that had married his Sister Salome, and out of a violent affection (unwilling any should enjoy her after him) hee gave strict and private commaundement, that if hee were slaine, shee should be put to death. But he returned with much honour, yet found his Wife extreamely discontented, to whom Josephus had (meaning it for the best, to prove Herod loved her) revealed his charge.

So by Salomes accusation hee put Josephus to death, but was reconciled to Mariam, who still bare the death of her Friends exceeding hardly.

In this meane time Herod was againe necessarily to revisite Rome, for Cæsar having overthrowne Anthony his great friend, was likely to make an alteration of his Fortune.

In his absence, newes came to Jerusalem that Cæsar had put him to death, their willingnes it should be so, together with the likelyhood, gave this Rumor so good credit, as Sohemus that had suceeded Josephus charge, succeeded him likewise in revealing it. So at Herods returne which was speedy and unexpected, he found Mariam so farre from joye, that she shewed apparent signes of sorrow. Hee still desiring to winne her to a better humour, she being very unable to conceale her passion, fell to upbraiding him with her Brothers death. As they were thus debating, came in a fellow with a Cuppe of Wine, who hired by Salome, saide first, it was a Love potion, which Mariam desired to deliver to the King: but afterwards he affirmed that it was a poyson, and that Sohemus had tolde her somewhat, which procured the vehement hate in her.

The King hearing this, more moved with Jealousie of Sohemus, then with this intent of poyson, sent her away, and presently after by the instigation of Salome, she was beheaded. Which rashnes was afterward punished in him, with an intollerable and almost Frantike passion for her death.

ACTUS PRIMUS

SCÆNA PRIMA

MARIAM sola
How oft have I with publike voyce runne on?
To censure Romes last Hero for deceit:
Because he wept when Pompeis life was gone,
Yet when he liv'd, hee thought his Name too great.
But now I doe recant, and Roman Lord
Excuse too rash a judgement in a woman:
My Sexe pleads pardon, pardon then afford,

Mistaking is with us, but too too common.
Now doe I finde by selfe Experience taught,
One Object yeelds both griefe and joy:
You wept indeed, when on his worth you thought,
But joyd that slaughter did your Foe destroy.
So at his death your Eyes true droppes did raine,
Whom dead, you did not wish alive againe.
When Herod liv'd, that now is done to death,
Oft have I wisht that I from him were free:
Oft have I wisht that he might lose his breath,
Oft have I wisht his Carkas dead to see.
Then Rage and Scorne had put my love to flight,
That Love which once on him was firmely set:
Hate hid his true affection from my sight,
And kept my heart from paying him his debt.
And blame me not, for Herods Jealousie
Had power even constancie itselfe to change:
For hee by barring me from libertie,
To shunne my ranging, taught me first to range.
But yet too chast a Scholler was my hart,
To learn to love another then my Lord:
To leave his Love, my lessons former part,
I quickly learn'd, the other I abhord.
But now his death to memorie doth call,
The tender love, that he to Mariam bare:
And mine to him, this makes those rivers fall,
Which by an other thought unmoistned are.
For Aristobolus the lowlyest youth
That ever did in Angels shape appeare:
The cruell Herod was not mov'd to ruth,
Then why grieves Mariam Herods death to heare?
Why joy I not the tongue no more shall speake,
That yeelded forth my brothers latest dome:
Both youth and beautie might thy furie breake,
And both in him did ill befit a Tombe.
And worthy Grandsire ill did he requite,
His high Assent alone by thee procur'd,
Except he murdred thee to free the spright
Which still he thought on earth too long immur'd.
How happie was it that Sohemus maide [minde]
Was mov'd to pittie my distrest estate?
Might Herods life a trustie servant finde,
My death to his had bene unseparate.
These thoughts have power, his death to make me beare,
Nay more, to wish the newes may firmely hold:
Yet cannot this repulse some falling teare,
That will against my will some griefe unfold.
And more I owe him for his love to me,

The deepest love that ever yet was seene:
Yet had I rather much a milke-maide bee,
Then be the Monarke of Judeas Queene.
It was for nought but love, he wisht his end
Might to my death but the vaunt-currier prove:
But I had rather still be foe then friend,
To him that saves for hate, and kills for love.
Hard-hearted Mariam, at thy discontent,
What flouds of teares have drencht his manly face?
How canst thou then so faintly now lament,
Thy truest lovers death, a deaths disgrace:
I, now mine eyes you do begin to right
The wrongs of your admirer. And my Lord,
Long since you should have put your smiles to flight,
Ill doth a widowed eye with joy accord,
Why now me thinkes the love I bare him then,
When virgin freedome left me unrestraind:
Doth to my heart begin to creepe agen,
My passion now is far from being faind,
But teares flie backe, and hide you in your bankes,
You must not be to Alexandra seene:
For if my mone be spide, but little thankes
Shall Mariam have, from that incensed Queene.

SCÆNA SECUNDA

MARIAM. ALEXANDRA.

ALEXANDRA
What meanes these teares? My Mariam doth mistake,
The newes we heard did tell the Tyrants end:
What weepst thou for thy brothers murthers sake,
Will ever wight a teare for Herod spend?
My curse pursue his breathless trunke and spirit,
Base Edomite the damned Esaus heire:
Must he ere Jacobs child the crowne inherit?
Must he vile wretch be set in Davids chaire?
No Davids soule within the bosome plac'te,
Of our forefather Abram was asham'd:
To see his seat with such a toade disgrac'te,
That seat that hath by Judas race bene fain'd.
Thou fatall enemie to royall blood,
Did not the murther of my boy suffice,
To stop thy cruell mouth that gaping stood?
But must thou dim the mild Hircanus eyes?
My gratious father, whose too readie hand

Did lift this Idumean from the dust:
And he ungratefull catiffe did withstand,
The man that did in him most friendly trust.
What kingdomes right could cruell Herod claime,
Was he not Esaus Issue, heyre of hell?
Then what succession can he have but shame?
Did not his Ancestor his birth-right sell?
O yes, he doth from Edoms name derive,
His cruell nature which with blood is fed:
That made him me of Sire and sonne deprive,
He ever thirsts for blood, and blood is red.
Weepst thou because his love to thee was bent?
And readst thou love in crimson caracters?
Slew he thy friends to worke thy hearts content?
No: hate may justly call that action hers.
He gave the sacred Priesthood for thy sake,
To Aristobolus. Yet doomde him dead:
Before his backe the Ephod warme could make,
And ere the Myter setled on his head,
Oh had he given my boy no lesse then right,
The double oyle should to his forehead bring:
A double honour, shining doubly bright,
His birth annoynted him both Priest and King.
And say my father, and my sonne he slewe,
To royalize by right your Prince borne breath:
Was love the cause, can Mariam deeme it true,
That Mariam gave commandment for her death?
I know by fits, he shewd some signes of love,
And yet not love, but raging lunacie:
And this his hate to thee may justly prove,
That sure he hates Hercanus familie.
Who knowes if he unconstant wavering Lord,
His love to Doris had renew'd againe?
And that he might his bed to her afford,
Perchance he wisht that Mariam might be slaine.

NUN [MARIAM]
Doris, Alas her time of love was past,
Those coales were rakte in embers long agoe;
If Mariams love and she was now disgrast,
Nor did I glorie in her overthrowe.
He not a whit his first borne sonne esteem'd,
Because as well as his he was not mine.
My children onely for his owne he deem'd,
These boyes that did descend from royall line.
These did he stile his heyres to Davids throne,
My Alexander if he live, shall sit
In the Majesticke seat of Salamon.

To will it so, did Herod thinke it fit.

ALEXANDRA
Why? who can claime from Alexanders brood
That Gold adorned Lyon-guarded Chaire?
Was Alexander not of Davids blood?
And was not Mariam Alexanders heire?
What more then right could Herod then bestow,
And who will thinke except for more then right,
He did not raise them, for they were not low,
But borne to weare the Crowne in his despight:
Then send those teares away that are not sent
To thee by season, but by passions power:
Thine eyes to cheere, thy cheekes to smiles be bent,
And entertaine with joy this happy houre.
Felicitie, if when shee comes, she findes
A mourning habite, and a cheerless looke,
Will thinke she is not welcome to thy minde,
And so perchance her lodging will not brooke.
Oh keepe her whilest thou hast her, if she goe
She will not easily returne againe:
Full many a yeere have I indur'd in woe,
Yet still have sude her presence to obtaine:
And did not I to her as presents send
A Table, that best Art did beautifie
Of two, to whom Heaven did best feature lend,
To woe her love by winning Anthony
For when a Princes favour we doe crave,
We first their Mynions loves do seeke to winne:
So I, that sought Felicitie to have,
Did with her Mynion Anthony beginne,
With double flight I sought to captivate
The warlike lover, but I did not right:
For if my gift had borne but halfe the rate,
The Roman had beene over-taken quite.
But now he fared like a hungry guest,
That to some plenteous festivall is gone,
Now this, now that, hee deems to eate were best,
Such choice doth make him let them all alone.
The boyes large forehead first did fayrest seeme
Then glaunst his eye upon my Mariams cheeke:
And that without comparison did deeme,
What was in eyther but he most did leeke.
And thus distracted, eythers beauties might
Within the others excellence was drown'd:
Too much delight did bare him from delight,
For eithers love, the others did confound.
Where if thy portraiture had onely gone,

His life from Herod, Anthony had taken:
He would have loved thee, and thee alone,
And left the browne Egyptian cleane forsaken.
And Cleopatra then to seeke had bene,
So firme a lover of her wayned face:
Then great Anthonius fall we had not seene,
By her that fled to have him hold the chase.
Then Mariam in a Romans Chariot set,
In place of Cleopatra might have showne:
A mart of Beauties in her visage met,
And part in this, that they were all her owne.

MARIAM
Not to be Emprise of aspiring Rome,
Would Mariam like to Cleopatra live:
With purest body will I presse my Toome,
And wish no favours Anthony could give.

ALEXANDRA
Let us retire us, that we may resolve
How now to deale in this reversed state:
Great are th'affaires that we must now revolve,
And great affaires must not be taken late.

SCÆNA TERTIA

MARIAM. ALEXANDRA. SALOME.

SALOME
More plotting yet? Why? now you have the thing
For which so oft you spent your supliant breath:
And Mariam hopes to have another King,
Her eyes doe sparkle joy for Herods death.

ALEXANDRA
If she desir'd another King to have,
She might before she came in Herods bed
Have had her wish. More Kings then one did crave,
For leave to set a Crowne upon her head.
I think with more then reason she laments,
That she is freed from such a sad annoy:
Who ist will weepe to part from discontent,
And if she joy, she did not causelesse joy.

SALOME
You durst not thus have given your tongue the raine,

If noble Herod still remaind in life:
Your daughters betters farre I dare maintaine,
Might have rejoyc'd to be my brothers wife.

MARIAM
My betters farre, base woman t'is untrue,
You scarce have ever my superiors seene:
For Mariams servants were as good as you,
Before she came to be Judeas Queene.

SALOME
Now stirs the tongue that is so quickly mov'd,
But more then once your collor have I borne:
Your fumish words are sooner sayd then prov'd,
And Salomes reply is onely scorne.

MARIAM
Scorne those that are for thy companions held,
Though I thy brothers face had never seene,
My birth thy baser birth so farre exceld,
I had to both of you the Princesse bene.
Thou party Jew, and party Edomite,
Thou Mongrell: issu'd from rejected race,
Thy Ancestors against the Heavens did fight,
And thou like them wilt heavenly birth disgrace.

SALOME
Still twit you me with nothing but my birth,
What ods betwixt your ancestors and mine?
Both borne of Adam, both were made of Earth,
And both did come from holy Abrahams line.

MARIAM
I favour thee when nothing else I say,
With thy blacke acts ile not pollute my breath:
Else to thy charge I might full justly lay
A shamefull life, besides a husbands death.

SALOME
Tis true indeed, I did the plots reveale,
That past betwixt your favorites and you:
I ment not I, a traytor to conceale.
Thus Salome your Mynion Joseph slue.

MARIAM
Heaven, dost thou meane this Infamy to smother?
Let slandred Mariam ope thy closed eare:
Selfe guilt hath ever bene suspitious mother,

And therefore I this speech with patience beare.
No, had not Salomes unstedfast heart,
In Josephus stead her Constabarus plast
To free her selfe, she had not usde the art,
To slander haplesse Mariam for unchast.

ALEXANDRA
Come Mariam, let us goe: it is no boote
To let the head contend against the foote.

SALOME, Sola
Lives Salome, to get so base a stile
As foote, to the proud Mariam Herods spirit?
In happy time for her endured exile,
For did he live she should not misse her merit:
But he is dead: and though he were my Brother,
His death such store of Cinders cannot cast
My Coales of love to quench: for though they smother
The flames a while, yet will they out at last.
Oh blest Arabia, in best climate plast,
I by the Fruit will censure of the Tree:
Tis not in vaine, thy happy name thou hast,
If all Arabians like Silleus bee:
Had not my Fate bene too too contrary,
When I on Constabarus first did gaze,
Silleus had beene object to mine eye:
Whose lookes and personage must allyes amaze.
But now ill Fated Salome, thy tongue
To Constabarus by itselfe is tide:
And now except I doe the Ebrew wrong
I cannot be the faire Arabian Bride:
What childish lets are these? Why stand I now
On honourable points? Tis long agoe
Since shame was written on my tainted brow,
And certaine tis, that shame is honours foe.
Had I upon my reputation stood,
Had I affected an unspotted life,
Josephus vaines had still bene stuft with blood,
And I to him had liv'd a sober wife.
Then had I never cast an eye of love,
On Constabarus now detested face,
Then had I kept my thoughts without remouve
And blusht at motion of the least disgrace:
But shame is gone, and honour wipt away,

And Impudencie on my forehead fits:
She bids me worke my will without delay,
And for my will I will imploy my wits.
He loves, I love; what then can be the cause,
Keepes me for being the Arabians wife?
It is the principles of Moses lawes,
For Constabarus still remaines in life,
If he to me did beare as Earnest hate,
As I to him, for him there were an ease,
A separating bill might free his fate:
From such a yoke that did so much displease.
Why should such priviledge to man be given?
Or given to them, why bard from women then?
Are men then we in greater grace with Heaven?
Or cannot women hate as well as men?
He be the custome-breaker: and beginne
To shew my Sexe the way to freedomes doore,
And with an offring will I purge my sinne,
The lawe was made for none but who are poore.
If Herod had liv'd, I might to him accuse
My present Lord, But for the futures sake
Then would I tell the King he did refuse
The sonnes of Baba in his power to take.
But now I must divorce him from my bed,
That my Silleus may possesse his roome:
Had I not begd his life he had bene dead,
I curse my tongue the hindrer of his doome,
But then my wandring hearte to him was fast,
Nor did I dreame of chaunge: Silleus said,
He would be here, and see he comes at last,
Had I not nam'd him longer had he staid.

SCÆNA QUINTA

SALOME, SILLEUS.

SILLEUS
Well found faire Salome Judeas pride,
Hath thy innated wisedome found the way
To make Silleus deeme him deified,
By gaining thee a more then precious pray?

SALOME
I have devisde the best I can devise,
A more imperfect meanes was never found:
But what cares Salome, it doth suffice

If our indevours with their end be crown'd.
In this our land we have an ancient use,
Permitted first by our law-givers head:
Who hates his wife, though for no just abuse,
May with a bill divorce her from his bed.
But in this custom women are not free,
Yet I for once will wrest it, blame not thou
The ill I doe, since what I do'es for thee,
Though others blame, Silleus should allow.

SILLEUS
Thinkes Salome, Silleus hath a tongue
To censure her faire actions: let my blood
Bedash my proper brow, for such a wrong,
The being yours, can make even vices good:
Arabia joy, prepare thy earth with greene,
Thou never happie wert indeed till now:
Now shall thy ground be trod by beauties Queene,
Her foote is destin'd to depresse thy brow.
Thou shalt faire Salome command as much
As if the royall ornament were thine:
The weaknes of Arabias King is such,
The kingdome is not his so much as mine.
My mouth is our Obodas oracle,
Who thinkes not ought but what Silleus will?
And thou rare creature, Asias miracle,
Shalt be to me as its Obodas still.

SALOME
Tis not for glory I thy love accept,
Judea yeelds me honours worthy store:
Had not affection in my bosome crept,
My native country should my life deplore.
Were not Silleus he with home I goe,
I would not change my Palestine for Rome:
Much lesse would I a glorious state to shew,
Goe far to purchase an Arabian toome.

SILLEUS
Far be it from Silleus so to thinke,
I know it is thy gratitude requites
The love that is in me, and shall not shrinke
Till death doe sever me from earths delights.

SALOME
But whist; me thinkes the wolfe is in our talke,
Be gone Silleus, who doth here arrive?
Tis Constabarus that doth hither walke,

Ile find a quarrell, him from me to drive.

SILLEUS
Farewell, but were it not for thy commaund,
In his despight Silleus here would stand.

SCÆNA SEXTA

SALOME. CONSTABARUS.

CONSTABARUS
Oh Salome, how much you wrõg your name,
Your race, your country, and your husband most?
A straungers private conference is shame,
I blush for you, that have your blushing lost.
Oft have I found, and found you to my griefe,
Consorted with this base Arabian heere:
Heaven knowes that you have bin my comfort chiefe,
Then doe not now my greater plague appeare.
Now by the stately Carved edifice
That on Mount Sion makes so faire a show,
And by the Altar fit for sacrifice,
I love thee more then thou thy selfe doest know.
Oft with a silent sorrow have I heard
How ill Judeas mouth doth censure thee:
And did I not thine honour much regard,
Thou shouldst not be exhorted thus for mee.
Didst thou but know the worth of honest fame,
How much a vertuous woman is esteem'd,
Thou wouldest like hell eschew deserved shame,
And seeke to be both chast and chastly deem'd.
Our wisest Prince did say, and true he said,
A vertuous woman crownes her husbands head.

SALOME
Did I for this, upreare thy lowe estate?
Did I for this requitall begge thy life,
That thou hadst forfeited haples fate?
To be to such a thankles wretch the wife.
This hand of mine hath lifted up thy head,
Which many a day agoe had falne full lowe,
Because the sonnes of Baba are not dead,
To me thou doest both life and fortune owe.

CONSTABARUS
You have my patience often exercisde,

Use make my choller keepe within the bankes:
Yet boast no more, but be by me advisde,
A benefit upbraided, forfeits thankes:
I prethy Salome dismisse this mood,
Thou doest not know how ill it fits thy place:
My words were all intended for thy good,
To raise thine honour and to stop disgrace.

SALOME
To stop disgrace? take thou no care for mee,
Nay do thy worst, thy worst I set not by:
No shame of mine is like to light on thee,
Thy love and admonitions I defie.
Thou shalt no hower longer call me wife,
Thy jealousie procures my hate so deepe:
That I from thee doe meane to free my life,
By a divorcing bill before I sleepe.

CONSTABARUS
Are Hebrew women now transform'd to men?
Why do you not as well our battels fight,
And weare our armour? Suffer this, and then
Let all the world be topsie turved quite.
Let fishes graze, beastes, swine, and birds descend,
Let fire burne downewards whilst the earth aspires:
Let Winters heat and Summers cold offend,
Let Thistels growe on Vines, and Grapes on Briers,
Set us to Spinne or Sowe, or at the best
Make us Wood-hewers, Waters-bearing wights:
For sacred service let us take no rest,
Use us as Joshua did the Gibonites.

SALOME
Hold on your talke, till it be time to end,
For me I am resolv'd it shall be so:
Though I be first that to this course do bend,
I shall not be the last full well I know.

CONSTABARUS
Why then be witnesse Heav'n, the Judge of sinnes,
Be witnesse Spirits that eschew the darke:
Be witnesse Angels, witnesse Cherubins,
Whose semblance fits upon the holy Arke:
Be witnesse earth, be witnesse Palestine,
Be witnesse Davids Citie, if my heart
Did ever merit such an act of thine:
Or if the fault be mine that make us part,
Since mildest Moses friend unto the Lord,

Did worke his wonders in the land of Ham,
And slew the first-borne Babes without a sword,
In signe whereof we eate the holy Lambe:
Till now that fourteene hundred yeeres are past,
Since first the Law with us hath been in force:
You are the first, and will I hope, be last,
That ever sought her husband to divorce.

SALOME
I meane not to be led by president,
My will shall be to me in stead of Law.

CONSTABARUS
I feare me much you will too late repent,
That you have ever liv'd so void of awe:
This is Silleus love that makes you thus
Reverse all order: you must next be his.
But if my thoughts aright the cause discusse,
In winning you, he gaines no lasting blisse,
I was Silleus, and not long agoe
Josephus then was Constabarus now:
When you became my friend you prov'd his foe,
As now for him you breake to me your vowd.

SALOME
If once I lov'd you, greater is your debt:
For certaine tis that you deserved it not.
And undeserved love we soone forget,
And therefore that to me can be no blot.
But now fare ill my once beloved Lord,
Yet never more belov'd then now abhord.

CONSTABARUS
Yet Constabarus biddeth thee farewell.
Farewell light creature. Heaven forgive thy sinne:
My prophecying spirit doth foretell
Thy wavering thoughts doe yet but new beginne,
Yet I have better scap'd then Joseph did,
But if our Herods death had bene delayd,
The valiant youths that I so long have hid,
Had bene by her, and I for them betrayd.
Therefore in happy houre did Cæsar give
The fatall blow to wanton Anthony.
For had he lived, our Herod then should live,
But great Anthonius death made Herod dye.
Had he enjoyed his breath, not I alone
Had beene in danger of a deadly fall:
But Mariam had the way of perill gone,

Though by the Tyrant most belov'd of all.
The sweet fac'd Mariam as free from guilt
As Heaven from spots, yet had her Lord come backe
Her purest blood had bene unjustly spilt,
And Salome it was would worke her wracke.
Though all Judea yeeld her innocent,
She often hath bene neere to punishment.

CHORUS
Those mindes that wholy dote upon delight,
Except they onely joy in inward good,
Still hope at last to hop upon the right,
And so from Sand they leape in loathsome mud.
Fond wretches, seeking what they cannot finde,
For no content attends a wavering minde.
If wealth they doe desire, and wealth attaine,
Then wondrous faine would they to honor lep:
Of meane degree they doe in honor gaine,
They would but wish a little higher step.
   Thus step to step, and wealth to wealth they ad,
   Yet cannot all their plenty make them glad.

Yet oft we see that some in humble state,
Are chreefull, pleasant, happy, and content:
When those indeed that are of higher state,
With vaine additions do their thoughts torment.
   Th'one would to his minde his fortune binde,
   T'hother to his fortune frames his minde.

To with varietie is signe of griefe,
For if you like your state as now it is,
Why should an alteration bring reliefe?
Nay change would then be fear'd as losse of blis,
   That man is onely happy in his Fate,
   That is delighted in a setled state.

Still Mariam wisht she from her Lord were free,
For expectation of varietie:
Yet now she sees her wishes prosperous bee,
She grieves, because her Lord so soone did die.
   Who can those vast imaginations feede,
   Where in a propertie, contempt doth breede?

Were Herod now perchance to live againe,
She would againe as much be grieved at that:
All that she may, she ever doth disdaine,
Her wishes guide her to she knowes not what.
   And sad must be their lookes, their honor sower,

That care for nothing being in their power.

PHERORAS and **GRAPHINA**.

PHERORAS
T'Is true Graphina, now the time drawes nye
Wherin the holy Priest with hallowed right,
The happy long desired knot shall tie,
Pheroras and Graphina to unite;
How oft have I with lifted hands implor'd
This blessed houre, till now implord in vaine,
Which hath my wished libertie restor'd,
And made my subject selfe my owne againe,
Thy love faire Mayd upon mine eye doth sit,
Whose nature hot doth dry the moysture all,
Which were in nature, and in reason fit
For my monachall Brothers death to fall:
Had Herod liv'd, he would have pluckt my hand
From faire Graphinas Palme perforce: and tide
The same in hatefull and despised band,
For I had had a Baby to my Bride:
Scarce can her Infant tongue with easie voice
Her name distinguish to anothers care
Yet had he liv'd, his power, and not my choise
Had made me solembly the contract sweare.
Have I not cause in such a change to joy?
What? though she be my Neece, a Princesse borne,
Neere bloods without respect: high birth a toy.
Since Love can teach blood and kindreds scorne.
What booted it that he did raise my head,
To be his Realmes Copartner, Kingdomes mate,
Withall, he kept Graphina from my bed,
More wisht by me then thrice Judeas state.
Oh, could not he be skilful! Judge in love,
That doted upon his Mariams face?
He, for his passion, Doris did remove.
I needed not a lawfull Wife displace,
It could not be but he had power to judge,
But he that never grudg'd a Kingdomes share,
This well knowne happinesse to me did grudge:
And ment to be therein without compare.
Else had I bene his equall in loves hoast,

For though the Diadem on Mariams head
Corrupt the vulgar judgements, I will boast
Graphinas brow's as white, her cheekes as red.
Why speaks thou not faire creature? move thy tongue,
For Silence is a signe of discontent:
It were to both our loves too great a wrong
If now this hower do find thee sadly bent.

GRAPHINA

Mistake me not my Lord, too oft have I
Desir'd this time to come with winged feete,
To be inwrapt with griefe when tis too nie,
You know my wishes ever yours did meete:
If I be silent, tis no more but feare
That I should say too little when I speake:
But since you will my imperfections beare,
In spight of doubt I will my silence breake:
Yet might amazement tie my moving tongue,
But that I know before Pheroras minde,
I have admired your affection long:
And cannot yet therein a reason finde.
Your hand hath lifted me from lowest state,
To highest eminencie wondrous grace,
And me your hand-maid have you made your mate,
Though all but you alone doe count me base.
You have preserved me pure at my request,
Though you so weake a vassaile might constraine
To yeeld to your high will, then last not best
In my respect a Princesse you disdaine,
Then need not all these favours studie crave,
To be requited by a simple maide:
And studie still you know must silence have,
Then be my cause for silence justly waide,
But studie cannot boote nor I requite,
Except your lowly hand-maides steadfast love
And fast obedience may your mind delight,
I will not promise more then I can prove.

PHERORAS

That studie needs not let Graphina smile,
And I desire no greater recompence:
I cannot vaunt me in a glorious stile,
Nor shew my love in far-fetcht eloquence:
But this beleeve me, never Herods heart
Hath held his Prince-borne beautie famed wife
In neerer place then thou faire virgin art,
To him that holds the glory of his life.
Should Herods body leave the Sepulcher,

And entertaine the sever'd ghost againe:
He should not be my nuptiall hinderer,
Except he hindred it with dying paine.
Come faire Graphina, let us goe in state,
This wish-indeered time to celebrate.

CONSTABARUS and **BABUS SONNES.**

BABUS 1ST SONNE
Now valiant friend you have our lives redeem'd,
Which lives as sav'd by you, to you are due:
Command and you shall see your selfe esteem'd,
Our lives and liberties belong to you.
This twice sixe yeares with hazard of your life,
You have conceal'd us from the tyrants sword:
Though cruell Herods sister were your wife,
You durst in scorne of fear this grace afford.
In recompence we know not what to say,
A poore reward were thankes for such a merit,
Our truest friendship at your feete we lay,
The best requitall to a noble spirit.

CONSTABARUS
Oh how you wrong our friendship valiant youth,
With friends there is not such a word as det:
Where amitie is tide with bond of truth,
All benefits are there in common set,
Then is the golden age with them renew'd,
All names of properties are banisht quite:
Division, and distinction, are eschew'd:
Each hath to what belongs to others right.
And tis not sure so full a benefit,
Freely to give, as freely to require:
A bountious act hath glory following it,
They cause the glory that the act desire.
All friendship should the pattern imitate,
Of Jesses Sonne and valiant Jonathan:
For neither Soveraignes nor fathers hate,
A friendship fixt on vertue sever can.
Too much of this, tis written in the heart,
And need no amplifying with the tongue:
Now may you from your living tombe depart,
Where Herods life hath kept you overlong.
Too great an injury to a noble minde,

To be quicke buried, you had purchast fame,
Some yeares a goe, but that you were confinde.
While thousand meaner did advance their name.
Your best of life, the prime of all your yeares,
Your time of action is from you bereft.
Twelve winters have you overpast in feares:
Yet if you use it well, enough is left.
And who can doubt but you will use it well?
The sonnes of Babus have it by descent:
In all their thoughts each action to excell,
Boldly to act, and wisely to invent.

BABUS 2ND SONNE

Had it not like the hatefull cuckoe beene,
Whose riper age his infant nurse doth kill:
So long we had not kept ourselves unseene,
But Constabarus safely crost our will:
For had the Tyrant fixt his cruell eye,
On our concealed faces wrath had swaide
His justice so, that he had forst us die.
And dearer price then life we should have paid,
For you our truest friend had falne with us:
And we much like a house on pillers set,
Had cleane deprest our prop, and therefore thus
Our readie will with our concealment met.
But now that you faire Lord are daungerlesse,
The Sonnes of Baba shall their rigor show:
And prove it was not basenes did oppresse
Our hearts so long, but honour kept them low.

BABUS 1ST SONNE

Yet do I feare this tale of Herods death,
At last will prove a very tale indeed:
It gives me strongly in my minde, his breath
Will be preserv'd to make a number bleed:
I wish not therefore to be set at large,
Yet peril to my selfe I do not feare:
Let us for some daies longer be your charge,
Till we of Herods state the truth do heare.

CONSTABARUS

What art thou turn'd a coward noble youth,
That thou beginst to doubt, undoubted truth?

BABUS 1ST SONNE

Were it my brothers tongue that cast this doubt,
I fro his hart would have the question out:
With this keene fauchion, but tis you my Lord

Against whose head I must not lift a sword:
I am so tide in gratitude Constabarus believe
You have no cause to take it ill,
If any word of mine your heart did grieve,
The word discented from the speakers will,
I know it was not feare the doubt begun,
But rather valour and your care of me,
A coward could not be your fathers sonne,
Yet know I doubts unnecessarie be:
For who can thinke that in Anthonius fall,
Herod his bosome friend should scape unbrusde:
Then Cæsar we might thee an idiot call,
If thou by him should'st be so farre abusde.

BABUS 2ND SONNE
Lord Constab. let me tell you this,
Upon submission Cæsar will forgive:
And therefore though the tyrant did amisse,
It may fall out that he will let him live.
Not many yeares agone it is since I
Directed thither by my fathers care,
In famous Rome for twice twelve monthes did live,
My life from Hebrewes crueltie to spare,
There though I were but yet of boyish age,
I bent mine eye to marke, mine eares to heare.
Where I did see Octavious then a page,
When first he did to Julius sight appeare:
Me thought I saw such mildnes in his face,
And such a sweetnes in his lookes did grow,
Withall, commixt with so majesticke grace,
His Phismony his Fortune did foreshow:
For this I am indebted to mine eye,
But then mine eare receiv'd more evidence,
By that I knew his love to clemency,
How he with hottest choller could dispence.

CONSTABARUS
But we have more then barely heard the news,
It hath bin twice confirm'd. And though some tongue
Might be so false, with false report t'abuse,
A false report hath never lasted long.
But be it so that Herod have his life,
Concealement would not then a whit availe:
For certaine t'is, that she that was my wife,
Would not to set her accusation faile.
And therefore now as good the venture give,
And free our selves from blot of cowardise:
As show a pittifull desire to live,

For, who can pittie but they must despise?

BABUS 1ST SONNE
I yeeld, but to necessitie I yeeld,
I dare upon this doubt ingage mine arme:
That Herod shall againe this kingdome weeld,
And prove his death to be a false alarme.

BABUS 2ND SONNE
I doubt it too: God grant it be an error,
Tis best without a cause to be in terror:
And rather had I, though my soule be mine,
My soule should lie, then prove a true divine.

CONSTABARUS
Come, come, let feare goe seeke a dastards nest,
Undaunted courage lies in a noble brest.

SCÆNA TERTIA

DORIS and **ANTIPATER.**

DORIS
Your royall buildings bow your loftie side,
And scope to her that is by right your Queen:
Let your humilitie upbraid the pride
Of those in whom no due respect is seene:
Nine times have we with Trumpets haughtie sound,
And banishing sow'r Leaven from our taste:
Observ'd the feast that takes the fruit from ground.
Since I faire Citie did behold thee last,
So long it is since Mariams purer cheeke
Did rob from mine the glory. And so long
Since I returnd my native Towne to seeke:
And with me nothing but the sence of wrong.
And thee my Boy, whose birth though great it were,
Yet have thy after fortunes prov'd but poore:
When thou wert borne how little did I feare
Thou shouldst be thrust from forth thy Fathers doore.
Art thout not Herods right begotten Sonne?
Was not the hapless Doris, Herods wife?
Yes: ere he had the Hebrew kingdome wonne,
I was companion to his private life.
Was I not faire enough to be a Queene?
Why ere thou wert to me false Monarch tide,
My lake of beauty might as well be seene,

As after I had liv'd five yeeres thy Bride.
Yet then thine oath came powring like the raine,
Which all affirm'd my face without compare:
And that if thou might'st Doris love obtaine,
For all the world besides thou didst not care.
Then was I yong, and rich, and nobly borne,
And therefore worthy to be Herods mate:
Yet thou ungratefull cast me off with scorne,
When Heavens purpose raisd your meaner fate.
Oft have I begd for vengeance for this fact,
And with dejected knees, aspiring hands
Have prayd the highest power to inact
The fall of her that on my Trophee stands.
Revenge I have according to my will,
Yet where I wisht this vengeance did not light:
I wisht it should high-hearted Mariam kill.
But it against my whilome Lord did fight
With thee sweet Boy I came, and came to try
If thou before his bastards might be plac'd
In Herods royall seat and dignitie.
But Mariams infants here are onely grac'd,
And now for us there doth no hope remaine:
Yet we will not returne till Herods end
Be more confirmed, perchance he is not slaine.
So glorious Fortunes may my Boy attend,
For if he live, hee'll think it doth suffice,
That he to Doris shows such crueltie:
For as he did my wretched life dispise,
So doe I know I shall despised die.
Let him but prove as naturall to thee,
As cruell to thy miserable mother:
His crueltie shall not upbraided bee
But in thy fortunes. I his faults will smother.

ANTIPATER
Each mouth within the Citie loudly cries
That Herods death is certaine: therefore wee
Had best some subtill hidden plot devise,
That Mariams children might subverted bee,
By poisons drinke, or else by murtherous Knife,
So we may be advanc'd, it skils not how:
They are but Bastards, you were Herods wife,
And foule adultery blotteth Mariams brow.

DORIS
They are too strong to be by us remov'd,
Or else revenges foulest spotted face:
By our detested wrongs might be approv'd,

But weaknesse must to greater power give place.
But let us now retire to grieve alone,
For solitarines best fitteth mone.

SILLEUS and **CONSTABARUS**.

SILLEUS
Well met Judean Lord, the onely wight
Silleus wisht to see. I am to call
Thy tongue to strict account.

CONSTABARUS
For what despight
I ready am to heare, and answere all.
But if directly at the cause I gesse
That breeds this challenge, you must pardon me:
And now some other ground of fight professe,
For I have vow'd, vowes must unbroken be.

SILLEUS
What may be your expectation? let me know.

CONSTABARUS
Why? ought concerning Salom, my sword
Shall not be welded for a cause so low,
A blow for her my arme will scorne t'afford.

SILLEUS
It is for slandering her unspotted name,
And I will make thee in thy vowes despight,
Sucke up the breath that did my Mistris blame,
And swallow it againe to doe her right.

CONSTABARUS
I prethee give some other quarrell ground
To finde beginning, raile against my name:
Or strike me first, or let some scarlet wound
Inflame my courage, give me words of shame,
Doe thou our Moses sacred Lawes disgrace,
Deprave our nation, doe me some despight:
I'm apt enough to fight in any case,
But yet for Salome I will not fight.

SILLEUS

Nor I for ought but Salome: My sword
That owes his service to her sacred name:
Will not an edge for other cause afford,
In other fight I am not sore of fame.

CONSTABARUS
For her, I pitty thee enough already,
For her, I therefore will not mangle thee:
A woman with a heart so most unsteady,
Will of her selfe sufficient torture bee.
I cannot envy for so light a gaine,
Her minde with such unconstancie doth runne:
As with a word thou didst her love obtaine,
So with a word she will from thee be wonne.
So light as her possesstions for most day
Is her affections lost, to me tis knowne:
As good goe hold the winde as make her stay,
She never loves, but till she call her owne.
She meerly is a painted sepulcher,
That is both faire, and vilely foule at once:
Though on her out-side graces garnish her,
Her mind is fild with worse then rotten bones.
And ever readie lifted is her hand,
To aime destruction at a husbands throat:
For proofes, Josephus and my selfe do stand,
Though once on both of us, she seem'd to doat.
Her mouth though serpent-like it never hisses,
Yet like a Serpent, poysons where it kisses.s

SILLEUS
Well Hebrew well, thou bark'st but wilt not bite.

CONSTABARUS
I tell thee still for her I will not fight.

SILLEUS
Why then I call thee coward.

CONSTABARUS
From my heart
I give thee thankes. A cowards hatefull name,
Cannot to valiant mindes a blot impart,
And therefore I with joy receive the same.
Thou know'st I am no coward: thou wert by
At the Arabian battaile th'other day:
And saw'st my sword with daring valiancy,
Amongst the faint Arabians cut my way.
The blood of foes no more could let it shine,

And twas inameled with some of thine.
But now have at thee, not for Salome
I fight: but to discharge a cowards stile:
Here gins the fight that shall not parted be,
Before a soule or two indure exile.

SILLEUS
Thy sword hath made some windowes for my blood,
To shew a horred crimson phisnomie:
To breath for both of us me thinkes twere good,
The day will give us time enough to die

CONSTABARUS
With all my hart take breath, thou shalt have time,
And if thou list, a twelve month, let us end:
Into thy cheekes there doth a palenes clime,
Thou canst not from my sword thy selfe defend.
What needest thou for Salome to fight,
Thou hast her, and may'st keepe her, none strives for her:
I willingly to thee resigne my right,
For in my very soule I do abhorre her.
Thou seest that I am fresh, unwounded yet,
Then not for feare I do this offer make:
Thou art with losse of blood, to fight unfit,
For here is one, and there another take.

SILLEUS
I will not leave as long as breath remaines
Within my wounded body: spare your words,
My heart in bloods stead, courage entertaines,
Salomes love no place for feare affords.

CONSTABARUS
Oh could thy soule but prophesie like mine,
I would not wonder thou should'st long to die:
For Salome if I aright divine
Will be then death a greater miserie.

SILLEUS
Then list, Ile breath no longer.

CONSTABARUS
Do thy will,
I hateles fight, and charitably kill. I, I, they fight,
Pittie thy selfe Silleus, let not death
Intru'd before his time into thy hart:
Alas it is too late to feare, his breath
Is from his body now about to part,

How far'st thou brave Arabian?

SILLEUS
Very well,
My legge is hurt, I can no longer fight:
It onely grieves me, that so soone I fell,
Before faire Salomes wrongs I came to right.

CONSTABARUS
Thy wounds are lesse then mortall. Never feare,
Thou shalt a safe and quicke recoverie finde:
Come, I will thee unto my lodging beare,
I hate thy body, but I love thy minde.

SILLEUS
Thankes noble Jew, I see a courtious foe,
Sterne enmitie to friendship can no art:
Had not my heart and tongue engagde me so,
I would from thee no foe, but friend depart.
My heart to Salome is tide so fast,
To leave her love for friendship, yet my skill
Shall be imploy'd to make your favour last,
And I will honour Constabarus still.

CONSTABARUS
I ope my bosome to thee, and will take
Thee in, as friend and grieve for thy complaint:
But if we doe not expedition make,
Thy losse of blood I feare will make thee faint.

CHORUS
To heare a tale with eares prejudicate,
It spoiles the judgement, and corrupts the senses.
That humane error given to every state,
Is greater enemie to innocence.
  It makes us foolish, heddy, rash, unjust,
  It makes us never try before we trust.

It will confound the meaning, change the words,
For it our sence of hearing much deceives
Besides no time to Judgement it affords,
To way the circumstance our eare receives.
  The ground of accidents it never tries,
  But makes us take for truth ten thousand lies.

Our eares and hearts are apt to hold for good,
That we our selves doe most desire to bee:
And then we drowne objections in the flood

Of partialitie, tis that we see
   That makes false rumours long with credit past,
   Though they like rumours must conclude at last.

The greatest part of us prejudicate,
With wishing Herods death do hold it true:
The being once deluded doth not bate,
The credit to a better likelihood due.
   Those few that wish it not the multitude,
   Doe carrie headlong, so they doubts conclude.

They not object the weake uncertaine ground,
Whereon they built this tale of Herods end:
Whereof the Author scarcely can be found,
And all because their wishes that way bend.
   They thinke not of the perill that ensu'th,
   If this should prove the contrary to truth.

On this same doubt, on this so light a breath,
They pawne their lives, and fortunes. For they all
Behave them as the newes of Herods death,
They did of most undoubted credit call:
   But if their actions now doe rightly hit,
   Let them commend their fortune, not their wit.

ACTUS TERTIUS

SCÆNA PRIMA

PHERORAS. SALOME.

PHERORAS
URge me no more Graphina to forsake,
Not twelve howers since I married her for love:
And doe you thinke a sisters power cane mak
A resolute decree, so soone remove?

SALOME
Poore minds they are that honour not affects.

PHERORAS
Who hunts for honour, happines neglects.

SALOME
You might have bene both of felicitie,
And honour too in equall measure seasde.

PHERORAS

It is not you can tell so well as I,
What tis can make me happie, or displeasde.

SALOME

To match for neither beautie nor respects
One meane of birth, but yet of meaner minde,
A woman full of naturall defects,
I wonder what your eye in her could finde.

PHERORAS

Mine eye found loveliness, mine eare found wit,
To please the one, and to enchant the other:
Grace on her eye, mirth on her tongue doth sit,
In lookes a child, in wisedomes house a mother.

SALOME

But say you thought her faire, as none thinks else,
Knowes not Pheroras, beautie is a blast:
Much like this flower which to day excels,
But longer then a day it will not last.

PHERORAS

Her with exceeds her beautie.

SALOME

Wit may show
The way to ill, as well as good you know.

PHERORAS

But wisedome is the porter of her head,
And bares all wicked words from issuing thence.

SALOME

But of a porter, better were you sped,
If she against their entrance made defence.

PHERORAS

But wherefore comes the sacred Ananell,
That hitherward his hastie steppes doth bend?
Great sacrificer y'are arrived well,
Ill newes from holy mouth I not attend.

SCÆNA SECUNDA

PHERORAS. SALOME. ANANELL.

ANANELL
My lippes, my sonne, with peacefull tidings blest,
Shall utter Honey to your listning eare:
A word of death comes not from Priestly brest,
I speake of life: in life there is no feare.
And for the newes I did the Heavens salute,
And fill'd the Temple with my thankfull voice:
For though that mourning may not me pollute,
At pleasing accidents I may rejoyce.

PHERORAS
Is Herod then reviv'd from certaine death?

SALOME
What? can your news restore my brothers breath?

ANANELL
Both so, and so, the King is safe and sound,
And did such grace in royall Cæsar meet:
That he with larger stile then ever crownd,
Within this houre Jerusalem will greet.
I did but come to tell you, and must backe
To make preparatives for sacrifice:
I knew his death, your hearts like mine did racke,
Though to conceale it, prov'd you wise.

SALOME
How can my joy sufficiently appeare?

PHERORAS
A heavier tale did never pierce mine eare.

SALOME
Now Salome of happinesse may boast.

PHERORAS
But now Pheroras is in danger most.

SALOME
I shall enjoy the comfort of my life.

PHERORAS
And I shall loose it, loosing of my wife.

SALOME
Joy heart, for Constabarus shall be slaine.

PHERORAS

Grieve soule, Graphina shall from me be tane.

SALOME

Smile cheekes, for the faire Silleus shall be mine.

PHERORAS

Weepe eyes, for I must with a child combine.

SALOME

Well brother, cease your mones, on one condition
Ile undertake to winne the Kings consent:
Graphina still shall be in your tuition,
And her with you be nere the lesse content.

PHERORAS

What's the condition? let me quickly know,
That I as quickly your command may act:
Were it to see what Hearbs in Ophir grow,
Or that the lofty Tyrus might be sackt.

SALOME

Tis no so hard a taske: It is no more,
But tell the King that Constabarus hid
The sonnes of Baba, done to death before:
And tis no more then Constabarus did.
And tell him more that he for Herods sake,
Not able to endure his brothers foe:
Did with a bill our separation make,
Though loth from Constabarus else to goe.

PHERORAS

Beleeve this tale for told, Ile goe from hence,
In Herods eare the Hebrew to deface:
And I that never studied eloquence,
Doe meane with eloquence this tale to grace.

[Exit.

SALOME

This will be Constabarus quicke dispatch,
Which from my mouth would lesser credit finde:
Yet shall he not decease without a match,
For Mariam shall not linger long behinde.
First Jealousie, if that availe not, feare
Shal be my minister to worke her end;
A common error moves not Herods eare,

Which doth so firmly to his Mariam bend.
She shall be charged with so horrid crime,
As Herods feare shall turne his love to hate:
Ile make some sweare that she desires to clime,
And seekes to poyson him for his estate,
I scorne that she should live my birth t'upbraid,
To call me base and hungry Edomite:
With patient show her choller I betrayd,
And watcht the time to be reveng'd by slite.
Now tongue of mine with scandall load her name,
Turne hers to fountaines, Herods eyes to flame:
Yet first I will begin Pheroras suite,
That he my earnest businesse may effect:
And I of Mariam will keepe me mute,
Till first some other doth her name detect.
Who's there, Silleus man? How fares your Lord?
That your aspects doe beare the badge of sorrow?

SILLEUS'S MAN
He hath the marks of Constabarus sword,
And for a while desires your sight to borrow.

SALOME
My heavy curse the hatefull sword pursue,
My heavier curse on the more hatefull arme
That wounded my Silleus. But renew
Your tale againe. Hath he no mortall harme?

SILLEUS'S MAN
No signe of danger doth in him appeare,
Nor are his wounds in place of perill seene:
Hee bides you be assured you need not feare,
He hopes to make you yet Arabias Queene.

SALOME
Commend my heart to be Silleus charge,
Tell him, my brothers suddaine comming now:
Will give my foote no roome to walke at large,
But I will see him yet ere night I vow.

SCÆNA TERTIA

MARIAM and **SOHEMUS.**

MARIAM
Sohemus, tell me what the newes may be

That makes your eyes so full, your cheekes so blew?

SOHEMUS
I know not how to call them. Ill for me
Tis sure they are: not so I hope for you.
Herod

MARIAM
Oh, what of Herod?

SOHEMUS
Herod lives.

MARIAM
How! lives? What in some Cave or forrest hid?

SOHEMUS
Nay, backe return'd with honor. Cæsar gives
Him greater grace then ere Anthonius did.

MARIAM
Foretell the ruine of my family,
Tell me that I shall see our Citie burnd:
Tell me I shall a death disgracefull die,
But tell me not that Herod is returnd.

SOHEMUS
Be not impatient Madam, be but milde,
His love to you againe will soone be bred:

MARIAM
I will not to his love be reconcilde,
With solemne vowes I have forsworne his Bed.

SOHEMUS
But you must breake those vowes.

MARIAM
Ile rather breake
The heart of Mariam. Cursed is my Fate:
But speake no more to me, in vaine ye speake
To live with him I so profoundly hate.

SOHEMUS
Great Queene, you must to me your pardon give,
Sohemus cannot now your will obey:
If your command should me to silence drive,
It were not to obey, but to betray.

Reject, and slight my speeches, mocke my faith,
Scorne my observance, call my counsell nought:
Though you regard not what Sohemus saith,
Yet will I ever freely speake my thought.
I feare ere long I shall faire Mariam see
In wofull state, and by her selfe undone:
Yet for your issues sake more temp'rate bee,
The heart by affabilitie is wonne.

MARIAM
And must I to my Prison turne againe?
Oh, now I see I was an hypocrite:
I did this morning for his death complaine,
And yet doe mourne, because he lives ere night.
When I his death beleev'd, compassion wrought,
And was the stickler twixt my heart and him:
But now that Curtaine's drawne from off my thought,
Hate doth appeare againe with visage grim:
And paints the face of Herod in my heart,
In horred colours with detested looke:
Then feare would come, but scorne doth play her part,
And faith that scorne with feare can never brooke.
I know I could inchaine him with a smile:
And lead him captive with a gentle word,
Scorne my looke should ever man beguile,
Or other speech, then meaning to afford.
Else Salome in vaine might spend her winde,
In vaine might Herods mother whet her tongue:
In vaine had they complotted and combinde,
For I could overthrow them all ere long.
Oh what a shelter is mine innocence,
To shield me from the pangs of inward griefe:
Gainst all mishaps it is my faire defence,
And to my sorrowes yeelds a large reliefe.
To be commandresse of the triple earth,
And sit in safetie from a fall secure:
To have all nations celebrate my birth,
I would not that my spirit were impure.
Let my distressed state unpittied bee,
Mine innocence is hope enough for mee.

[Exit.

SOHEMUS
Poore guiltlesse Queene. Oh that my wish might place
A little temper now about thy heart:
Unbridled speech is Mariams worst disgrace,
And will indanger her without desart.

I am in greater hazard. O're my head,
The fatall axe doth hang unstedily:
My disobediance once discovered,
Will shake it downe: Sohemus so shall die.
For when the King shall find, we thought his death
Had bene as certaine as we see his life:
And markes withall I slighted so his breath,
As to preserve alive his matchles wife.
Nay more, to give to Alexanders hand
The regall dignitie. The soveraigne power,
How I had yeelded up at her command,
The strength of all the citie, Davids Tower.
What more then common death may I expect,
Since I too well do know his crueltie:
Twere death, a word of Herods to neglect,
What then to doe directly contrarie?
Yet life I quite thee with a willing spirit,
And thinke thou could'st not better be imploi'd:
I forfeit thee for her that more doth merit,
Ten such were better dead then she destroi'd.
But fare thee well chast Queene, well may I see
The darknes palpable, and rivers part:
The sunne stand still. Nay more retorted bee,
But never woman with so pure a heart.
Thine eyes grave majestie keepes all in awe,
And cuts the winges of every loose desire:
Thy brow is table to the modest lawe,
Yet though we dare not love, we may admire.
And if I die, it shall my soule content,
My breath in Mariams service shall be spent.

CHORUS
TIs not enough for one that is a wife
To keepe her spotles from an act of ill:
But from suspition she should free her life,
And bare her selfe of power as well as will.
   Tis not so glorious for her to be free,
   As by her proper selfe restrain'd to bee.

When she hath spatious ground to walke upon,
Why on the ridge should she desire to goe?
It is no glory to forbeare alone,
Those things that may her honour overthrowe.
   But tis thanke-worthy, if she will not take
   All lawfull liberties for honours sake.

That wife her hand against her fame doth reare,
That more then to her Lord alone will give

A private word to any second eare,
And though she may with reputation live.
    Yet though most chast, she doth her glory blot,
    And wounds her honour, though she killes it not.

When to their Husbands they themselves doe bind,
Doe they not wholy give themselves away?
Or give they but their body not their mind,
Reserving that though best, for others pray?
    No sure, their thoughts no more can be their owne,
    And therefore should to none but one be knowne.

Then she usurpes upon anothers right,
That seekes to be by publike language grac't:
And though her thoughts reflect with purest light,
Her mind if not peculiar is not chast.
    For in a wife it is no worse to finde,
    A common body, then a common minde.

And every mind though free from thought of ill,
That out of glory seekes a worth to show:
When any's eares but one therewith they fill,
Doth in a sort her pureness overthrow.
    Now Mariam had, (but that to this she bent)
    Beene free from feare, as well as innocent.

ACTUS QUARTUS

SCÆNA PRIMA

Enter **HEROD** and his **ATTENDANTS**.

HEROD
Haile happie citie, happie in thy store,
And happy that thy buildings such we see:
More happie in the Temple where w'adore,
But most of all that Mariam lives in thee.
Art thou return'd? how fares my Mariam?

[Enter **NUNITO**.

NUNITO
She's well my Lord, and will anon be here
As you commanded.

HEROD

Muffle up thy browe,
Thou daies darke taper. Mariam will appeare.
And where she shines, we need not thy dimme light,
Oh hast thy steps rare creature, speed thy pace:
And let thy presence make the day more bright,
And cheere the heart of Herod with thy face.
It is an age since I from Mariam went,
Me thinkes our parting was in Davids daies:
The houres are so increast by discontent,
Deepe sorrowe, Joshua like the season staies:
But when I am with Mariam,time runnes on,
Her sight, can make months, minutes, daies of weeke:
An hower is then no sooner come then gon.
When in her face mine eye for wonders seekes.
You world commanding citie, Europes grace,
Twice hath my curious eye your streets survai'd,
And I have seene the stature filled place,
That once if not for griefe had bene betrai'd.
I all your Roman beauties have beheld,
And seene the showes your Ediles did prepare,
I saw the sum of what in you exceld,
Yet saw no miracle like Mariam rare.
The faire and famous Livia, Cæsarslove,
The worlds commanding Mistresse did I see:
Whose beauties both the world and Rome approve,
Yet Mariam: Livia, is not like to thee.
Be patient but a little, while mine eyes
Within your compast limits be contain'd:
That object straight shall your desires suffice,
From which you were so long a while restrain'd.
How wisely Mariam doth the time delay,
Least suddaine joy my fence should suffocate:
I am prepar'd, thou needst no longer stay:
Whose there, my Mariam, more then happie fate?
Oh no, it is Pheroras, welcome Brother,
Now for a while, I must my passion smother.

SCÆNA SECUNDA

HEROD. PHERORAS.

PHERORAS
All health and safetie waite upon my Lord,
And may you long in prosperous fortunes live
With Rome commanding Cæsar, at accord,
And have all honors that the world can give.

HEROD

Oh brother, now thou speakst not from thy hart,
No, thou hast strooke a blow at Herods love:
That cannot quickly from my memory part,
Though Salome did me to pardon move.
Valiant Phasaelus, now to thee farewell,
Thou wert my kinde and honorable brother:
Oh hapless houre, when you selfe stricken fell,
Thou fathers Image, glory of thy mother.
Had I desir'd a greater sute of thee,
Then to withhold thee from a harlots bed,
Thou wouldst have granted it: but now I see
All are not like that in a wombe are bred.
Thou wouldst not, hadst thou heard of Herods death,
Have made his buriall time, thy bridall houre:
Thou wouldst with clamours, not with joyfull breath,
Have show'd the newes to be not sweet but soure.

PHERORAS

Phasaelus great worth I know did staine
Pheroras petty valour: but they lie
(Excepting you your selfe) that dare maintaine,
That he did honor Herod more then I,
For what I show'd, loves power constraind me show,
And pardon loving faults for Mariams sake.

HEROD

Mariam, where is she?

PHERORAS

Nay, I do not know,
But absent use of her faire name I make:
You have forgiven greater faults then this,
For Constabarus that against you will
Preserv'd the sonnes of Baba, lives in blisse,
Though you commanded him the youths to kill.

HEROD

Goe, take a present order for his death,
And let those traytors feele the worst of feares:
Now Salome will whine to begge his breath,
But Ile be deafe to prayers: and blind to teares.

PHERORAS

He is my Lord from Salome divorst,
Though her affection did to leave him grieve:
Yet was she by her love to you inforst,

To leave the man that would your foes relieve.

HEROD
Then haste them to their death. I will requite
Thee, gentle Mariam. Salome, I meane
The thought of Mariam doth so steale my spirit,
My mouth from speech of her I cannot weane.

[Exit.

SCÆNA TERTIA

HEROD. MARIAM.

HEROD
And heere she comes indeed: happily met
My best, and deerest halfe: what ailes my deare?
Thou doest the difference certainly forget
Twixt Duskey habits, and a time so cleare.

MARIAM
My Lord, I suit my garment to my minde,
And there no cheerfull colours can I finde.

HEROD
Is this my welcome? have I longd so much
To see my dearest Mariam discontent?
What ist that is the cause thy heart to touch?
Oh speake, that I thy sorrow may prevent.
Art thou not Juries Queene, and Herods too?
Be my Commandres. be my Soveraigne guide:
To be by thee directed I will woo,
For in thy pleasure lies my highest pride.
Or if thou think Judeas narrow bound,
Too strict a limit for thy great command:
Thou shalt be Empresse of Arabia crownd,
For thou shalt rule, and I will winne the Land.
Ile robbe the holy Davids Sepulcher
To give thee wealth, if thou for wealth do care:
Thou shalt have all, they did with him inter,
And I for thee will make the Temple bare.

MARIAM
I neither have of power nor riches want,
I have enough, nor doe I wish for more:
Your offers to my heart no ease can grant,

Except they could my brothers life restore.
No, had you wisht the wretched Mariam glad,
Or had your love to her bene truly tide:
Nay, had you not desir'd to make her sad,
My brother nor my Grandsyre had not dide.

HEROD
Wilt thou beleeve no oathes to cleere thy Lord?
How oft have I with execration sworne:
Thou art by me belov'd, by me ador'd,
Yet are my protestations heard with scorne.
Hircanus plotted to deprive my head
Of this long setled honor that I weare:
And therefore I did justly doome him dead,
To rid the Realme from perill, me from feare,
Yet I for Mariams sake doe so repent
The death of one: whose blood she did inherit:
I wish I had a Kingdomes treasure spent,
So I had nere expeld Hircanus spirit.
As I affected that same noble youth,
In lasting infamie my name inrole:
If I not mournd his death with heartie truth.
Did I not shew to him my earnest love,
When I to him the Priesthood did restore?
And did for him a living Priest remove,
Which never had bene done but once before.

MARIAM
I know that mov'd by importunitie,
You made him Priest, and shortly after die.

HEROD
I will not speake, unles to be beleev'd,
This froward humor will not doe you good:
It hath too much already Herod griev'd.
To thinke that you on termes of hate have stood.
Yet smile my dearest Mariam, doe but smile,
And I will all unkind conceits exile.

MARIAM
I cannot frame disguise, nor never taught
My face a looke dissenting from my thought.

HEROD
By heav'n you vexe me, build not on my love.

MARIAM
I wil not build on so unstable ground.

HEROD
Nought is so fixt, but peevishnes may move.

MARIAM
Tis better sleightest cause then none were found.

HEROD
Be judge your selfe, if ever Herod sought
Or would be mov'd a cause of change to finde:
Yet let your looke declare a milder thought,
My heart againe you shall to Mariam binde.
How oft did I for you my Mother chide.
Revile my Sister, and my brother rate:
And tell them all my Mariam they belide,
Distrust me still, if there be signes of hate.

SCÆNA QUARTA

HEROD
What hast though here?

BU
A drinke procuring love,
The Queene desir'd me to deliver it.

MARIAM
Did I: some hatefull practise this will prove,
Yet can it be no worse then Heavens permit.

HEROD
Confesse the truth thou wicked instrument,
To her outrageous will, tis passion sure:
Tell true, and thou shalt scape the punishment,
Which if thou doe conceale thou shalt endure.

BU
I know not, but I doubt it be no lesse,
Long since the hate of you her heart did cease.

HEROD
Know'st thou the cause thereof?

BU
My Lord I gesse,
Sohemus told the tale that did displease.

HEROD

Oh heaven! Sohemus false! Goe let him die,
Stay not to suffer him to speake a word:
Oh damned villaine, did he falsifie
The oath he swore ev'n of his owne accord?
Now doe I know thy falshood, painted Divill
Thou white Inchantress. Oh thou art so foule,
That Ysop cannot clense thee worst of evill.
A beauteous body hides a loathsome soule,
Your love Sohemus mov'd by his affection,
Though he have ever heretofore bene true:
Did blab forsooth, that I did give direction,
If we were put to death to slaughter you.
And you in black revenge attended now
To adde a murther to your breach of vow.

MARIAM

Is this a dream?

HEROD

Oh Heaven, that t'were no more,
Ile give my Realme to who can prove it so:
Would I were like any begger poore,
So I for false my Mariam did not know.
Foule pith contain'd in the fairest rinde,
That ever grac'd a Cæder. Oh thine eye
Is pure as heaven, but impure thy minde,
And for impuritie shall Mariam die.
Why didst thou love Sohemus?

MARIAM

They can tell
That say I lov'd him, Mariam saies not so.

HEROD

Oh cannot impudence the coales expell,
That for thy love in Herods bosome glow?
It is as plaine as water, and deniall
Makes of thy falsehood but a greater triall.
Hast thou beheld thy selfe, and couldst thou staine
So rare perfection: even for love of thee
I doe profoundly hate thee. Wert thou plaine,
Thou shoul'dst the wonder of Judea bee.
But oh thou art not. Hell it selfe lies hid
Beneath thy heavenly show. Yet never were thou chast:
Thou might'st exalt, pull downe, command, forbid,
And be above the wheele of fortune plast.

Hadst thou complotted Herods massacre,
That so thy sonne a Monarch might be stilde,
Not halfe so grievous such an action were,
As once to thinke, that Mariam is defilde.
Bright workmanship of nature sulli'd ore,
With pitched darknes now thine end shall bee:
Thou shalt not live faire fiend to cozen more,
With heavy semblance, as thou cousnedst mee.
Yet must I love thee in diespight of death,
And thou shalt die in the dispight of love:
For neither shall my love prolong thy breath,
Nor shall thy losse of breath my love remove.
I might have seene thy falsehood in thy face,
Where coul'dst thou get thy stares that serv'd for eyes?
Except by theft, and theft is foule disgrace:
This had appear'd before were Herod wise,
But I'me a sot, a very sot, no better.
My wisedome long agoe a wandring fell,
Thy face incountring it, my wit did fetter,
And made me for delight my freedome sell,
Give me my heart false creature, tis a wrong.
My guiltless heart should now with thine be slaine:
Thou hadst no right to looke it up so long,
And with usurpers name I Mariam staine.

[Enter **BU**.

HEROD
Have you design'd Sohemus to his end?

BU
I have my Lord.

HEROD
Then call our royall guard
To doe as much for Mariam, they offend
Leave ill unblam'd, or good without reward.
Here take her to her death Come back, come backe,
What ment I to deprive the world of light:
To muffle Jury in the foulest blacke,
That ever was an opposite to white.
Why wither would you carrie her:

SOULDIER
You bad
We should conduct her to her death my Lord.

HEROD

Wie sure I did not, Herod was not mad,
Why should she feele the furie of the sword?
Oh now the griefe returnes into my heart,
And pulles me peecemeale: love and hate doe fight:
And now hath bove [love] acquir'd the greater part,
Yet now hath hate, affection conquer'd quite.
And therefore beare her hence: and Hebrew why
Seize you with Lyons paws the fairest lam
Of all the flocke? She must not, shall not, die,
Without her I most miserable am.
And with her more then most, away, away,
But beare her but to prison, not to death:
And is she gon indeed, stay villaines stay,
Her lookes alone preserv'd your Soveraignes breath.
Well let her goe, but yet she shall not die,
I cannot thinke she ment to poison me:
But certaine tis she liv'd too wantonly,
And therefor shall she never more be free.

SCÆNA QUINTA

BU

Foule villanie, can thy pitchie coloured soule
Permit thine eare to heare her caules doome?
And not inforce thy tongue that tale controule,
That must unjustly bring her to her toome.
Oh Salome thou hast thy selfe repaid,
For all the benefits that thou hast done:
Thou art the cause I have the queene betraid,
Thou hast my hart to darkest false-hood wonne.
I am condemn'd, heav'n gave me not my tongue
To slander innocents, to lie, deceive:
To be the hatefull instrument to wrong,
The earth of greatest glory to bereave.
My sinne ascends and doth to heav'n crie,
It is the blackest deed that ever was:
And there doth record it it downe in leaves of brasse.
Oh how my heart doth quake: Achitophel,
Thou found a means thy selfe from shame to free:
And sure my soule approves thou didst not well,
All follow some, and I will follow thee.

SCÆNA SEXTA

CONSTABARUS, BABUS SONNES, and their **GUARD.**

CONSTABARUS
Now here we step our last, the way to death,
We must not tread this way a second time:
Yet let us resolutely yeeld our breath,
Death is the onely ladder, Heav'n to clime.

BABUS 1ST SONNE
With willing mind I could my selfe resigne,
But yet it grieves me with a griefe untold:
Our death should be accompani'd with thine,
Our friendship we to thee have dearely fold.

CONSTABARUS
Still wilt thou wrong the sacred name of friend?
Then should'st thou never stile it friendship more:
But base mechanicke traffique that doth lend,
Yet will be sure they shall the debt restore.
I could with needlesse complement returne,
Tis for thy ceremonie I could say:
Tis I that made the fire your house to burne,
For but for me she would not you betray.
Had not the damned woman sought mine end,
You had not bene the subject of her hate:
You never did her hatefull minde offend,
Nor could your deaths have freed your nuptiall fate.
Therefore faire friends, though you were still unborne,
Some other subtiltie devisde should bee:
Were by my life, though guiltles should be torne,
Thus have I prov'd, tis you that die for mee.
And therefore should I weakely now lament,
You have but done your duties, friends should die:
Alone their friends disaster to prevent,
Though not compeld by strong necessitie.
But now farewell faire citie, never more
Shall I behold your beautie shining bright:
Farewell of Jewish men the worthy store,
But no farewell to any female wight.
You wavering crue: my curse to you I leave,
You had but one to give you any grace:
And you your selves will Mariams life bereave,
Your common-wealth doth innocencie chase.
You creatures made to be the humane curse,
You Tygers, Lyonnesses, hungry Beares,
Teare massacring Hienas: nay far worse,
For they for pray doe shed their fained teares.
But you will weepe, (you creature crosse to good)

For your unquenched thirst of humane blood:
You were the Angels cast from heav'n for pride,
And still doe keepe your Angels outward show,
But none of you are inly beautifide,
For still your heav'n depriving pride doth grow.
Did not the sinnes of many require a scourge,
Your place on earth had bene by this withstood:
But since a flood no more the world must purge,
You staid in office of a second flood.
You giddy creatures, sowers of debate,
You'll love to day, and for no other cause,
But for you yesterday did deply hate,
You are the wreake of order, breach of lawes.
You best, are foolish, froward, wanton, vaine,
Your worst adulterous, murderous, cunning proude
And Salome attends the latter traine,
Or rather he their leader is allowd.
I do the sottishnesse of men bewaile,
That doe with following you inhance your pride:
T'were better that the humane race should faile,
Then be by such a mischiefe multiplide.
Chams servile curse to all your sexe was given,
Because in in Paradise you did offend:
Then doe we not resist the will of Heaven,
When on your willes like servants we attend?
You are to nothing constant but to ill,
You are with nought but wickednesse indude:
You loves are set on nothing but your will,
And thus my censure I of you conclude.
You are the least of goods, the worst of evils,
Your best are worse then men: your worst then divels.

BABUS 2ND SONNE
Come let us to our death: are we not blest?
Our death will freedome from these creatures give:
Those trouble quiet sowers of unrest,
And this I vow that had I leave to live,
I would for ever lead a single life,
And never venture on a divellish wife.

SCÆNA SEPTIMA

HEROD and **SALOME**.

HEROD
Nay, she shall die. Die quoth you, she shall:

But for the meanes. The meanes! Methinks tis hard
To finde a meanes to murther her withall,
Therefore I am resolv'd she shall be spar'd.

SALOME
Why? let her be beheaded.

HEROD
That were well,
Thinke you that swords are miracles like you:
Her skinne will ev'ry Curtlax edge refell,
And then your enterprise you well may rue.
What if the fierce Arabian notice take,
Of this your wretched weaponlesse estate:
They answere when we bid resistance make,
That Mariams skinne their fanchions did rebate.
Beware of this, you make a goodly hand,
If you of weapons doe deprive our Land.

SALOME
Why drowne her then.

HEROD
Indeed a sweet device,
Why? would not ev'ry River turn her course
Rather then doe her beautie prejudice?
And be reverted to the proper sourse.
So not a drop of water should be found
In all Judeas quondam firtill ground.

SALOME
Then let the fire devoure her.

HEROD
T'will not bee:
Flame is from her deriv'd into my heart:
Thou nursest flame, flame will not murther thee,
My fairest Mariam, fullest of desert.

SALOME
Then let her live for me.

HEROD
Nay, she shall die,
But can you live without her?

SALOME
doubt you that?

HEROD
I 'me sure I cannot. I beseech you trie:
I have experience but I know not what.

SALOME
How should I try?

HEROD
Why let my love be slaine
But if we cannot live without her sight
Youle finde the meanes to make her breathe againe,
Or else you will bereave my comfort quite.

SALOME
Oh I: I warrant you.

HEROD
What is she gone?
And gone to bid the world be overthrowne:
What? is her hearts composure hardest stone?
To what a passe are cruell women growne?
She is return'd already: have you done?
Ist possible you can command so soone?
A creatures heart to quench the flaming Sonne,
Or from the skie to wipe away the Moone.

SALOME
If Mariam be the Sunne and Moone, it is:
For I already have commanded this.

HEROD
But have you seene her cheek?

SALOME
A thousand times,

HEROD
But did you mark it too?

SALOME
I very well.

HEROD
What ist?

SALOME
A Crimson bush, that ever limes

The soule whose foresight doth not much excell.

HEROD
Send word she shall not dye. Her cheek a bush,
Nay, then I see indeed you mark it not.

SALOME
Tis very faire, but yet will never blush,
Though foule dishonors do her forehead blot.

HEROD
Then let her die, tis very true indeed,
And for this fault alone shall Mariam bleed.

SALOME
What fault my Lord?

HEROD
What fault ist? You that aske:
If you be ignorant I know of none.
To call her backe from death shall be your taske,
I'm glad that she for innocent is knowne.
For on the brow of Mariam hangs a Fleece,
Whose slenderest twine is strong enough to binde
The hearts of Kings, the pride and shame of Greece,
Troy flaming Helens not so fairely shinde.

SALOME
Tis true indeed, she layes them out for nets,
To catch the hearts that doe not shune a baite:
Tis time to speake: for Herod sure forgets
That Mariams very tresses hide deceit.

HEROD
Oh doe they so? nay, then you doe but well,
In sooth I thought it had beene haire:
Nets call you them? Lord, how they doe excell,
I never saw a net that show'd so faire.
But have you heard her speake?

SALOME
You know I have.

HEROD
And were you not amaz'd?

SALOME
No, not a whit.

HEROD
Then t'was not her you heard, her life Ile save,
For Mariam hath a world amazing wit.

SALOME
She speaks a beauteous language, but within
Her heart is false as powder: and her tongue
Doth but allure the auditors to sinne,
And is the instrument to doe you wrong.

HEROD
It may be so: nay, tis so: shee's unchaste,
Her mouth will ope to ev'ry strangers eare:
Then let the executioner make haste,
Lest she inchant him, if her words he heare.
Let him be deafe, lest she do him surprise
That shall to free her spirit be assignde:
Yet what boots deafenes if he have his eyes,
Her murthererr must be both deafe and blinde.
For if he see, he needs must see the starres
That shine on eyther side of Mariams face:
Whose sweet aspect will terminate the warres,
Wherewith he should a soule so precious chase.
Her eyes can speake, and in their speaking move,
Oft did my heart with reverence receive
The worlds mandates. Pretty tales of love
They utter, which can humane bondage weave.
But shall I let this heavens modell dye?
Which for a small selfe-portraiture she drew:
Her eyes like starres, her forehead like the skie,
She is like Heaven, and must be heavenly true.

SALOME
Your thoughts do rave with doating on the Queen,
Her eyes are ebon hewde, and you'll confesse:
A sable starre hath beene but seldome seene,
Then speake of reason more, of Mariam lesse.

HEROD
Your selfe are held a goodly creature heere,
Yet so unlike my Mariam in your shape:
That when to her you have approached neere,
My selfe hath often tane you for an Ape.
And yet you prate of beautie: goe your waies,
You are to her a Sun burnt Blackamore:
Your paintings cannot equall Mariams praise,
Her nature is so rich, you are so poore.

Let her be staide from death, for if she die,
We do we know not what to stop her breath:
A world cannot another Mariam buy,
Why stay you lingring? countermaund her death.

SALOME
Then youle no more remember what hath past,
Sohemus love, and hers shall be forgot:
Tis well in truth: that fault may be her last,
And she may mend, though yet she love you not.

HEROD
Oh God: tis true. Sohemus: earth and heav'n,
Why did you both conspire to make my curst:
In cousning me with showes, and proofes unev'n?
She show'd the best, and yet did prove the worst.
Her show was such, as had our singing king
The holy David, Mariams beautie seene:
The Hittits had then felt no deadly sting,
Not Bethsabe had never bene a Queene.
Or had his sonne the wisest man of men,
Whose fond delight did most consist in change
Beheld her face, he had bene staid agen,
No creature having her, can wish to range.
Had Asuerus seene my Mariams brow,
The humble Jewe, she might have walkt alone:
Her beauteous vertue should have staid below,
Whiles Mariam mounted to the Persian throne.
But what availes it all: for in the waight
She is deceitfull, light as vanitie:
Oh she was made for nothing but a bait,
To traine some haples man to miserie.
I am the haples amn that have bene trainde,
To endles bondage, I will see her yet:
Me thinkes I should discerne her if she fainde.
Can humane eyes be dazde by womans wit?
Once more these eyes of mine with hers shall meet,
Before the headsman doe her life bereave:
Shall I for ever part from thee my sweet?
Without the taking of my latest leave.

SALOME
You had as good resolve to save her now,
Ile stay her death, tis well determined:
For sure she never more will breake her vow,
Sohemus and Josephus both are dead.

HEROD

She shall not live, nor will I see her face,
A long heald wound, a second time doth bleed:
With Joseph I remember her disgrace,
A shamefull end ensues a shamefull deed.
Oh that I had not cald to minde anew,
The discontent of Mariams wavering hart:
Twas you: you foule mouth'd Ate, none but you,
That did the thought hereof to me impart.
Hence from my sight, my blacke tormenter hence,
For hadst not thou made Herod unsecure:
I had not doubted Mariams innocence,
But still had helf her in my heart for pure.

SALOME
Ile leave you to your passion: tis no time
To purge me now, though of a guiltless crime.

[Exit.

HEROD
Destruction take thee: thou hast made my hart
As heavie as revenge, I am so dull,
Methinkes I am not sensible of smart,
Though hiddious horrors at my bosome pull.
My head waies downwards: therefore will I goe
To try if I can sleepe away my woe.

SCÆNA OCTAVA

MARIAM
Am I the Mariam that presum'd so much,
And deem'd my face must needes preserve my breath?
I, I it was that thought my beautie such,
At it alone could countermaund my death.
Now death will teach me: he can pale as well
A cheeke of roses, as a cheeke lesse bright:
And dim an eye whose shine doth most excell,
As soone as one that casts a meaner light.
Had not my selfe against my selfe conspirde,
No plot: no adversarie from without
Could Herods love from Mariam have retirde,
Or from his heart have thrust my semblamce out.
The wanton Queene that never lov'd for love,
False Cleopatra, wholly set on gaine:
With all her slights did prove: yet vainly prove,
For her the love of Herod to obtaine.

Yet her allurements, all her courtly guile,
Her smiles, her favours, and her smooth deceit
Could not my face from Herods minde exile,
But were with him of lesse then little weight.
That face and person that in Asia late
For beauties Goddesse Paphos Queene was tane:
That face that did captive great Julius fate,
That very face that was Anthonius bane.
That face that to be Egipts pride was borne,
That face that all the world esteem'd so rare:
Did Herod hate, despise, neglect, and scorne,
When with the same, he Mariams did compare.
This made that I improvidently wrought,
And on the wager even my life did pawne:
Because I thought, and yet but truly thought,
That Herods love could not from me be drawne.
But now though out of time, I plainly see
It could be drawne, though never drawne from me:
Had I but with humilitie bene grac'te,
As well as faire I might have prov'd me wise:
But I did thinke because I knew me chaste,
One vertue for a woman, might suffice.
That mind for glory of our sexe might stand,
Wherein humilitie and chastitie
Doth march with equall paces hand in hand,
But one if single seene, who setteth by?
And I had singly one, but tis my joy,
That I was ever innocent, though sower:
And therefore can they but my life destroy,
My Soule is free from adversaries power.

[Enter **DORIS**.

You Princes great in power, and high in birth,
Be great and high, I envy not your hap:
Your birth must be from dust: your power on earth,
In heav'n shall Mariam sit in Saraes lap.

DORIS
I heav'n, your beautie cannot bring you thither,
Your soule is blacke and spotted, full of sinne:
You in adultry liv'd nine yeare together,
And heav'n will never let adultry in.

MARIAM
What art thou that doest poore Mariam pursue?
Some spirit sent to drive me to dispaire:
Who sees for truth that Mariam is untrue,

If faire she be, she is as chaste as faire.

DORIS
I am that Doris that was once belov'd,
Belov'd by Herod: Herods lawfull wife:
Twas you that Doris from his side remov'd,
And rob'd from me the glory of my life.

MARIAM
Was that adultry: did not Moses say,
That he that being matcht did deadly hate:
Might by permission put his wife away,
And take a more belov'd to be his mate?

DORIS
What did he hate me for: for simple truth?
For bringing beautious babes for love to him:
For riches: noble birth, or tender youth,
Of for no staine did Doris honour dim?
Oh tell me Mariam, tell me if you knowe,
Which fault of these made Herod Doris foe.
These thrice three years have I with hands held up,
And bowed knees fast nailed to the ground:
Besought for thee the dreggs of that same cup,
That cup of wrath that is for sinners found
And now thou are to drinke it: Doris curse,
Upon thy selfe did all this while attend,
But now it shall pursue thy children worse.

MARIAM
Oh Doris now to thee my knees I bend,
That hart that never bow'd to thee doth bow:
Curse not mine infants, let it thee suffice,
That Heav'n doth punishment to me allow.
Thy curse is cause that guiltles Mariam dies.

DORIS
Had I ten thousand tongues, and ev'ry tongue
Inflam'd with poisons power and steept in gall:
My curses would not answere for my wrong,
Though I in cursing thee imployed them all.
Heare thou that didst mount Gerarim command,
To be a place whereon with cause to curse:
Stretch thy revenging arme: thrust forth thy hand,
And plague the mother much: the children worse.
Throw flaming fire upon the baseborne heads
That were begotten in unlawful beds.
But let them live till they have sence to know

What tis to be in miserable state:
Then be their neerest friends their overthrow,
Attended be they by suspitious hate.
And Mariam, I doe hope this boy of mine
Shall one day come to be the death of thine.

[Exit.

MARIAM
Oh! Heaven forbid. I hope the world shall see,
This curse of thine shall be return'd on thee:
Now earth farewell, though I be yet but yong,
Yet I, me thinks, have knowne thee too too long.

[Exit.

CHORUS
The fairest action of our humane life,
Is scorning to revenge an injurie:
For who forgives without a further strife,
His adversaries heart to him doth tie.
And tis a firmer conquest truely fed,
To winne the heart, then overthrow the head.

If we a worthy enemie doe finde.
To yeeld to worth, it must be nobly done:
But if of baser mettall be his minde,
In base revenge there is no honor wonne.
Who would a worthy courage overthrow,
And who would wrastle with a worthles foe?

We say our hearts are great and cannot yeeld,
Because they cannot yeeld it proves them poore:
Great hearts are task't beyond their power, but feld
The weakest Lyon will the lowdest roare.
Truths schoole for certaine doth this same allow,
High hartednes doth sometimes teach to bow.

A noble heart doth teach a vertuous scorne,
To scorne to owe a dutie over-long:
To scorne to be for benefits forborne,
To scorne to lie, to scorne to doe a wrong.
  To scorne to beare an injurie in minde,
  To scorne a free-borne heart slave-like to binde.

But if for wrongs we needs revenge must have,
Then be our vengeance of the noblest kinde:
Doe we his body from our furie save,

And let our hate prevaile against our minde?
   What can gainst him a greater vengeance bee,
   Then make his foe more worthy farre then hee?

Had Mariam scorn'd to leave a due unpaide,
Shee would to Herod then have paid her love:
And not have bene by sullen passion swaide
To fixe her thoughts all injurie above
   Is vertuous pride. Had Mariam thus bene prou'd,
   Long famous life to her had bene allowd.

ACTUS QUINTUS

SCÆNA PRIMA

NUNITO
When, sweetest friend, did I so farre offend
Your heavenly selfe: that you my fault to quit
Have made me now relator of her end,
The end of beautie? Chastitie and wit,
Was none so haples in the fatall place,
But I, most wretched, for the Queene t'chuse,
Tis certaine I have some ill boding face
That made me culd to tell this luckles newes.
And yet no news to Herod: were it new,
To him unhappy t'had not bene at all:
Yet doe I long to come within his vew,
That he may know his wife did guiltles fall:
And heere he comes. Your Mariam greets you well.

[Enter **HEROD**.

HEROD
What? lives my Mariam? joy, exceeding joy.
She shall not die.

NUNITO
Heav'n doth your will repell.

HEROD
Oh doe not with thy words my life destroy,
I prethy tell no dying-tale: thine eye
Without thy tongue doth tell but too too much:
Yet let thy tongues addition make me die,
Death welcome, comes to him whose griefe is such.

NUNITO

I went amongst the curious gazing troope,
To see the last of her that was the best:
To see if death had hart to make her stoope,
To see the Sunne admiring Phœnix next.
When there I came, upon the way I saw
The stately Mariam not debas'd by feare:
Her looke did seeme to keepe the world in awe,
Yet mildly did her face this fortune beare.

HEROD

Thou dost usurpe my right, my tongue was fram'd
To be the instrument of Mariams praise:
Yet speake: she cannot be too often fam'd:
All tongues suffice not her sweet name to raise.

NUNITO

But as she came she Alexandra met,
Who did her death (sweet Queene) no whit bewaile,
But as if nature she did quite forget.
She did upon her daughter loudly raile.

HEROD

Why stopt you not her mouth? where had she words
To darke that, that Heaven made so bright?
Our sacred tongue no Epithite affords,
To call her other then the worlds delight.

NUNITO

Shee told her that her death was too too good,
And that already she had liv'd too long:
She said, she sham'd to have a part in blood
Of her that did the princely Herod wrong.

HEROD

Base picke-thanke Divell. Shame, twas all her glory,
That she to noble Mariam was the mother:
But never shall it live in any storie
Her name, except to infamy ile smother.
What answere did her princely daughter make?

NUNITO

She made no answere, but she lookt the while,
As if thereof she scarce did notive take,
Yet smilde, a dutifull, though scornefull smile.

HEROD

Sweet creature, I that looke to mind doe call,

Full oft hath Herod bene amaz'd withall.

NUNITO
Go on, she came unmov'd with pleasant grace,
As if to triumph her arrivall were:
In stately habite, and with cheerfull face:
Yet ev'ry eye was moyst, but Mariams there.
When justly opposite to me she came,
She pickt me out from all the crue:
She beckned to me, cald me by my name,
For she my name, my birth, and fortune knew.

HEROD
What did she name thee? happy, happy man,
Wilt thou not ever love that name the better?
But what sweet tune did this faire dying Swan
Afford thine care: tell all, omit no letter.

NUNITO
Tell thou my Lord, said she.

HEROD
Mee, ment she mee?
Ist true, the more my shame: I was her Lod,
Were I not made her Lord, I still should bee:
But now her name must be by me adord.
Oh say, what said she more? each word she sed
Shall be the food whereon my heart is fed.

NUNITO
Tell thou my Lord thou saw'st me loose my breath.

HEROD
Oh that I could that sentence now controule.

NUNITO
If guiltily eternall be my death,

HEROD
I hold her chast ev'n in my inmost soule.

NUNITO
By three daies hence if wishes could revive,
I know himselfe would make me oft alive.

HEROD
Three daies: three houres, three minutes, not so much
A minute in a thousand parts divided,

My penitencie for her death is such,
As in the first I wisht she had not died.
But forward in thy tale.

NUNITO
Why on she went,
And after she some silent praier had sed
She did as if to die she were content,
And thus to heav'n her heav'nly soule is fled.

HEROD
But art thou sure there doth no life remaine?
Ist possible my Mariam should be dead,
Is there no tricke to make her breathe againe?

NUNITO
Her body is divided from her head.

HEROD
Why yet me thinkes there might be found by art,
Strange waies of cure, tis sure rare things are don:
By an inventive head, and willing heart.

NUNITO
Let not my Lord your fancies idlely run.
It is as possible it should be seene,
That we should make the holy Abraham live,
Though he intomb'd two thousand yeares had bene,
As breath againe to slaughtred Mariam give.
But now for more assaults prepare your eares,

HEROD
There cannot be a further cause of mone,
This accident shall shelter me from feares:
What can I feare? already Mariams gone.
Yet tell ev'n what you will:

NUNITO
As I came by,
From Mariams death I saw upon a tree,
A man that to his necke a cord did tie:
Which cord he had designd his end to bee.
When me he once discern'd, he downwards bow'd.
And thus with fearefull voyce she cride alowd,
Goe tell the King he trusted ere he tride,
I am the cause that Mariam causeles dide.

HEROD

Damnation take him, for it was the slave
That said she ment with poisons deadly force
To end my life that she the Crowne might have:
Which tale did Mariam from her selfe divorce.
Oh pardon me thou pure unspotted Ghost,
My punishment must needes sufficient bee,
In missing that content I valued most:
Which was thy admirable face to see.
I had but one inestimable Jewell,
Yet one I had no monarch had the like.
And therefore may I curse my selfe as cruell:
Twas broken by a blowe my selfe did strike.
I gaz'd thereon and never thought me blest,
But when on it my dazled eye might rest:
A pretious Mirror made by wonderous art,
I prized it ten times dearer then my Crowne,
And laide it up fast foulded in my heart:
Yet I in suddaine choler cast it downe.
And pasht it all to peeces: twas no foe,
That robd me of it, no Arabian host,
Nor no Armenian guide hath usde me so.
But Herods wretched selfe hath Herod crost.
She was my gracefull moytie, me accurst,
To slay my better halfe and save my worst.
But sure she is not dead you did but jest,
To put me in perplexitie a while,
Twere well indeed if I could so be drest:
I see she is alive, me thinkes you smile.

NUNITO
If sainted Abel yet deceased bee,
Tis certaine Mariam is as dead as hee.

HEROD
Why then goe call her to me, bid her now
Put on faire habite, stately ornament:
And let no frowne oreshade her smoothest brow,
In her doth Herod place his whole content.

NUNITO
Sheel come in stately weedes to please your sence,
If now she come attirde in robe of heaven:
Remember you your selfe did send her hence,
And now to you she can no more be given.

HEROD
Shee's dead, hell take her murderers, she was faire,
Oh what a hand she had, it was so white,

It did the whitenes of the snowe impaire:
I never more shall see so sweet a sight.

NUNITO
Tis true, her hand was rare.

HEROD
Her hand? her hands;
She had not singly one of beautie rare,
But such a paire as heere where Herod stands,
He dares the world to make to both compare.
Accursed Salome, hadst thou bene still.
My Mariam had bene breathing by my side:
Oh never had I: had I had my will,
Sent forth command, that Mariam should have dide.
But Salome thou didst with envy vexe,
To see thy selfe out-matched in thy sexe:
Upon your sexes forehead Mariam sat,
To grace you all like an imperiall crowne,
But you fond foole have rudely pusht thereat,
And proudly puld your proper glory downe.
One smile of hers: Nay, not so much a looke
Was worth a hundred thousand such as you,
Judea how canst thou the wretches brooke.
That robd from thee the fairest of the crew?
You dwellers in the now deprived land,
Wherein the matchles Mariam was bred:
Why graspe not each of you a sword in hand,
To ay me at me your cruell Soveraignes head.
Oh when you thinke of Herod as your King.
And owner of the pride of Palestine:
This act to your remembrance likewise bring,
Tis I have overthrowne your royall line.
Within her purer vaines the blood did run,
That from her Grandam Sara she deriv'd,
Whose beldame age the love of Kings hath wonne,
Oh that her issue had as long bene li'vd.
But can her eye be made by death obscure?
I cannot thinke but it must sparkle still:
Foule sacriledge to rob those lights so pure,
From out a Temple made by heav'nly skill.
I am the Villaine that have done the deed,
The cruell deed, though by anothers hand,
My word though not my sword made Mariam bleed,
Hircanus Grandchild did at my command.
That Mariam that I once did love so deare,
The partner of my now detested bed,
Why shine you sun with an aspect so cleare?

I tell you once againe my Mariams dead.
You could but shine, if some Egyptian blows,
Or Æthiopian doudy lose her life:
This was, then wherefore bend you not your brows,
The King of Juries fair and spotles wife.
Denie thy beames, and Moone refuse thy light,
Let all the starres be darke, let Juries eye
No more distinguish which is day and night:
Since her best birth did in her bosome die.
Those fond Idolaters the men of Greece,
Maintaine these orbes are safely governed:
That each within themselves have Gods a peece,
By whom their stedfast course is justly led,
But were it so, as so it cannot bee,
They all would put their mourning garments on:
Not one of them would yeeld a light to mee,
To me that is the cause that Mariams gon.
For though they fame their Saturne melancholy,
Of sowre behaviours, and of angry moode.
They fame him likewise to be just and holy,
And justice needes must seeke revenge for blood.
Their Jove, if Jove he were, would sure desire.
To punish him that slew so faire a lasse:
For Ledaes beautie set his heart on fire,
Yet she not halfe so faire as Mariam was.
And Mars would deeme his Venus had bene slaine,
Sol to recover her would never sticke:
For if he want the power her life to gaine:
Then Physicks God is but an Empericke.
The Queene of love would storme for beauties sake,
And Hermes too, since he bestow'd her wit,
The nights pale light for angrie griefe would shake,
To see chast Mariam die in age unfit.
But oh I am deceiv'd, she past them all
In every gift, in every propertie:
Her Excellencies wrought her timeless fall,
And they rejoyc'd, not griev'd to see her die.
The Paphian Goddesse did repent her wast,
When she to one such beautie did allow:
Mercurius thought her wit his wit surpast,
And Cinthia envi'd Mariams brighter brow.
But these are ficitons, they are voyd of sence,
The Greekes but dreame, and dreaming falsehoods tell:
They neither can offend nor give defence,
And not by them it was my Mariam fell.
If she had bene like an Egiptian blacke,
And not so faire, she had bene longer livde:
Her overflow of beautie turned backe,

And drownde the spring from whence it was derivde.
Her heav'nly beautie twas that made me thinke
That it with chastitie could never dwell:
But now I see that heavn'n in her did linke,
A spirit and a person to excell.
Ile muffle up my selfe in endles night,
And never let mine eyes behold the light.
Retire thy selfe vile monster, worse then hee
That staind the virgin earth with brothers blood,
Still in some vault or denne inclosed bee,
Where with thy teares thou maist beget a flood,
Which flood in time may drowne thee: happie day
When thou at once shalt die and finde a grave,
A stone upon the vault, some one shall lay,
Which monument shall an inscription have.
And these shall be the words it shall containe,
Heere Herod lies, that hath his Mariam slaine.

CHORUS
Who ever hath beheld with steadfast eye,
The strange events of this one onely day:
How many were deceiv'd? How many die,
That once to day did grounds of safetie lay?
    It will from them all certaintie bereve,
    Since twice sixe houres so many can deceive.

This morning Herod held for surely dead.
And all the Jewes on Mariam did attend:
And Constabarus rise from Saloms bed,
And neither dreamd of a divorce or end.
    Pheroras joyd that he might have his wife,
    And Babus sonnes for safetie of their life.

To night our Herod doth alive remaine.
The guiltles Mariam is depriv'd of breath:
Stout Constabarus both divorst and slaine,
The valiant sonnes of Baba have their death.
    Pheroras sure his love to be bereft,
    If Salome her sute unmade had left.

Herod this morning did expect with joy.
To see his Mariams much beloved face:
And yet ere night he did her life destroy,
And surely thought she did her name disgrace.
    Yet now againe so short do humors last,
    He both repents her death and knowes her chast.

Had he with wisdome now her death delaide,

He at his pleasure might command her death:
But now he hath his power so much betraide,
As all his woes cannot restore her breath.
   Now doth he strangely lunatickly rave,
   Because his Mariams life he cannot save.

This daies events were certainly ordainde,
To be the warning to posteritie:
So many changes are therein containde,
So admirablie strange varietie.
   This day alone, our sagest Hebrewes shall
   In after times the schoole of wisedome call.

LADY ELIZABETH CARY – A CONCISE BIBLIOGRAPHY

Other than the 'Tragedy of Mariam' and 'The History of the Life, Reign and Death of Edward II', much of her original work has been lost, including most of her poetry.

The Mirror of the World, a translation of Abraham Ortelius's Le mirroir du monde (1598)
The Tragedy of Mariam, the Fair Queen of Jewry (pub. 1613)
Reply of the Most Illustrious Cardinal of Perron (1630)
The History of the Life, Reign and Death of Edward II, or The History of the most Unfortunate Prince, King Edward II (pub. 1680)

www.ingramcontent.com/pod-product-compliance
Lightning Source LLC
Chambersburg PA
CBHW021941040426
42448CB00008B/1185